P9-CMT-691

Animal Math
Adding with Ants

Tracey Steffora

Heinemann
LIBRARY
Chicago, Illinois

© 2014 Heinemann Library
an imprint of Capstone Global Library, LLC
Chicago, Illinois

To contact Capstone Global Library please phone 800-747-4992, or visit our web site, www.capstonepub.com

All rights reserved. No part of this publication may be reproduced or transmitted in any form or by any means, electronic or mechanical, including photocopying, recording, taping, or any information storage and retrieval system, without permission in writing from the publisher.

Edited by Daniel Nunn, Abby Colich, and Sian Smith
Designed by Joanna Hinton-Malivoire
Picture research by Elizabeth Alexander
Production by Victoria Fitzgerald
Originated by Capstone Global Library Ltd
Printed in the United States of America in North Mankato, Minnesota

072014
008309RP

Library of Congress Cataloging-in-Publication Data
Steffora, Tracey.

Adding with ants / Tracey Steffora.
    pages cm.—(Animal Math)
Includes bibliographical references and index.

ISBN 978-1-4329-7558-6 (hb)
ISBN 978-1-4329-7565-4 (pb)
1. Addition—Juvenile literature. 2. Counting—Juvenile literature. I. Title.
  QA115.S777 2014
  513.2'11—dc23   2012049396

Acknowledgments
The author and publisher are grateful to the following for permission to reproduce copyright material: iStockphoto pp.12, 19 (© arlindo71); Photoshot p.22 (A.N.T. Photo Library/NHPA); Shutterstock pp. 4 (© Micha Klootwijk), 5 (© Mike VON BERGEN), 6, 7, 9 (© Eric Isselee), 8,9,10,11,13,15 (© Potapov Alexander, © Andrey Pavlov), 14, 15 (© Evgeniy Ayupov), 14, 15, 17, 19, 20 (© jps), 14, 15, 17 (© asharkyu).

Front and back cover photographs of forest ants reproduced with permission of Shutterstock (© Potapov Alexander). Front cover photograph of ants on grass reproduced with permission of Shutterstock (© Andrey Armyagov).

We would like to thank Elaine Bennett for her invaluable help in the preparation of this book.

Every effort has been made to contact copyright holders of any material reproduced in this book. Any omissions will be rectified in subsequent printings if notice is given to the publisher.

Contents

Some words are shown in bold, **like this**. You can find them in a glossary on page 23.

Aiding with Ants

Look at this leafcutter ant. It is carrying a leaf!

Ants work together as a group. When we want to know how many there are altogether in a group, we can **add** to find out. Let's add some ants!

Counting All Ants

One ant carries a leaf.

Here come two more ants.

1　　2　　3

Here are all the ants. How many are there altogether? Count and find out.

We can **add** to find out how many there are altogether.

One **plus** two is three.

There are three ants altogether.

1 + 2 = 3

Double the Ants!

Three ants are marching to the nest.

Along come three more! How many are there altogether?

3 + 3 = ?

Start with three ants.

Add three more.

Three **plus** three is six.

$$3 + 3 = 6$$

There are **double** the ants!

Counting on Ants

Six ants are marching through the forest.

Along come three more! How many
are there altogether?

We can **add** by counting on.

Start with six ants.

Count on three more.

$$6 + 3 = ?$$

Six **plus** three **equals** nine. There are nine ants altogether.

Counting on is a fast way to find out how many there are altogether.

6 + 3 = 9

Look! There are two ants on an **anthill**.

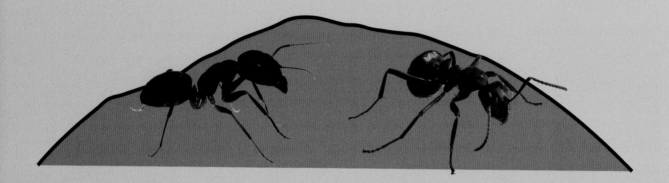

Now five ants are marching along to join them. How many are there altogether?

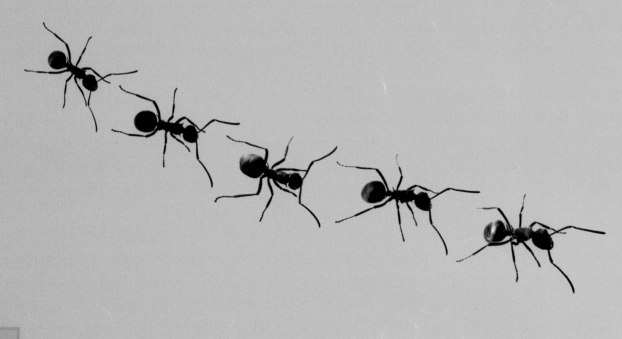

Start with two. Count on five times.

Two **plus** five **equals** seven.

$$2 + 5 = 7$$

We can **add** up numbers in any order.

Two **plus** five is seven.

$$2 + 5 = 7$$

Five plus two is also seven!

$$5 + 2 = 7$$

It is easier to count on when we start with the biggest number.

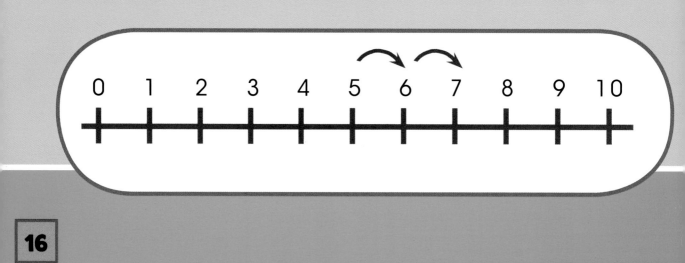

The nine ants in the forest keep marching along.

They join together with the seven ants on the **anthill**.

Now how many are there?

$$9 + 7 = ?$$

Start with nine.

Count on seven.

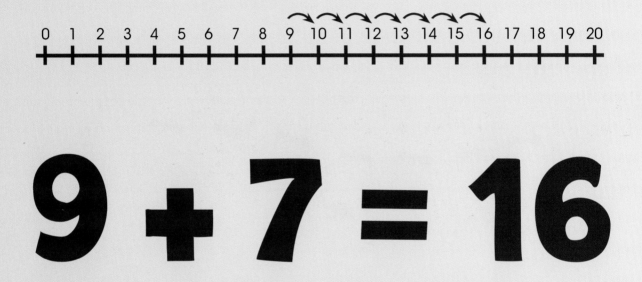

9 + 7 = 16

Nine **plus** seven **equals** sixteen. There are sixteen ants in total.

Sixteen ants! That is a **colony** of ants going into the nest!

Audition Chart

Look at the pattern of numbers on this chart. It can help us to **add** numbers.

Let's try it together. **6 + 3 = ?**

0	1	2	3	4	5	6	7	8	9
	2	3	4	5	6	7	8	9	10
	3	4	5	6	7	8	9	10	11
	4	5	6	7	8	9	10	11	12
	5	6	7	8	9	10	11	12	13
	6	7	8	9	10	11	12	13	14
	7	8	9	10	11	12	13	14	15
	8	9	10	11	12	13	14	15	16
	9	10	11	12	13	14	15	16	17
	10	11	12	13	14	15	16	17	18

Put one finger on the red six.

Put the other finger on the blue three.

Slide your fingers until they meet.

Now it's your turn!

What is seven **plus** four?

> Put one finger on the red seven.
>
> Put the other finger on the blue four.
>
> Slide your fingers until they meet.

$$7 + 4 = ?$$

Answer on page 22.

Ant Facts

- Ant nests are often underground and have many tunnels.

- The queen ant is the biggest ant in the **colony**. She lays all the eggs.

- The worker ants in the colony are all female.

- Ants are one of the strongest creatures alive. They can lift up many times their own body weight!

7 + 4 = 11

Answer

Math Glossary

add to put groups of things together and find out how many there are in all

double to have twice as much of something

equals = This sign says equals. You use it to show the answer.

plus + This sign says plus. You use it to add one number to another number.

Ant Glossary

anthill a mound made when ants dig their nest

colony a large group of something, such as ants

Teaching Notes

First, children must develop an understanding of quantity and what happens when quantities are combined. Then, they are able to further develop their mathematical knowledge concerning the operation of addition. This title supports this concept by putting together groups of objects (ants) and introducing the mathematical vocabulary and symbols of addition.

Use this title to further support core operations and algebraic thinking standards:

- While reading the book aloud to the class, engage groups of children to physically and visually "act" out the equations. Remember to reinforce language such as *add*, *altogether*, and *equal* when acting out each equation with the children.

- Group children in pairs and give each pair five similar objects (e.g., paper clips, counters, etc.). Ask them to put the five objects in two sets. Next, ask them to explore how many different ways they can make two sets of objects. Then, have them record their answers using drawings, numbers and symbols, or word sentences.

Related Common Core Standards

CCSS.Math.Content.K.OA.A.1   CCSS.Math.Content.1.OA.B.3

CCSS.Math.Content.K.OA.A.2   CCSS.Math.Content.1.OA.C.5

CCSS.Math.Content.1.OA.A.1   CCSS.Math.Content.1.OA.C.6

FREDERICK COUNTY PUBLIC LIBRARIES

OCT   2018   21982318751934